THE KINDERGARTEN IN JAPAN

The Kindergarten in Japan

ITS EFFECT
UPON THE PHYSICAL, MENTAL
AND MORAL TRAITS OF
JAPANESE SCHOOL
CHILDREN

BY

TSUNEKICHI MIZUNO
B. A. Hiroshima
Higher Normal School, Japan
1908

Boston
THE STRATFORD CO., Publishers

PREFACE

IN how far are the assumed virtues and promises
of educational theories and doctrines actually
realized when these theories and doctrines are
put into operation? This question is typical of the
most important problems that educational science is
today resolutely facing and attempting to solve. Just
as no educational doctrine is so old or so well established as to be immune to unbiased investigation, so
no proposal for reform should be looked upon as so
plausible as to claim immunity to the acid-test of
measured results. The ultimate effects of certain pro-
posals may be difficult to predict; the immediate effects may be difficult to determine and evaluate; but
these are assumptions neither to be made lightly nor
to be used as a cloak for mental inertia. The very
difficulty should rather be a spur to the devising of
means toward accurate prediction, exact measurement;
and just evaluation.

Mr. Mizuno's book records the results of an investigation into the influences of the educational theories
and doctrines underlying the kindergarten. It would
not be the part of wisdom either to condemn or to ap-

prove a highly involved theory upon the basis of a single investigation necessarily so limited as this; but such investigations may well point the way to more extended studies and suggest a method through the gradual refinement of which the basic facts may ultimately be revealed.

W. C. BAGLEY.

School of Education,
University of Illinois.

CONTENTS

CHAPTER I

CHAPTER II

CHAPTER III

CHAPTER IV

THE KINDERGARTEN
IN JAPAN

CHAPTER I

INTRODUCTION

"KINDERGARTEN" signifies a children's garden, or a garden of children. This name was selected by its founder, Friedrich Froebel, because it expressed his idea of development directed by a knowledge of the organism to be developed and aided by the selection of a right environment. But this name fails to express another important aspect of the institution; "the garden of children" gives no suggestion of its social aspect. According to the founder, the object of the kindergarten is as follows:—"It shall receive children before the school age, give them employment suited to their nature, strengthen their bodies, exercise their senses, employ their waking mind, make them acquainted judiciously with nature and society, cultivate especially the heart and temper, and lead them to the foundation of all living." He was unable for a long time to find a suitable name. He called the institution "a school for the psychological training of little children by means of play and occupations." At one time he called it "the children's in-

[11]

stitution", or "Play School". He would often exclaim, "Ah! How I wish I could find a name for my youngest born!" He was once walking over the hills towards Blankenburg with Middendorff and Barop. Suddenly he stopped and shouted joyfully, "Eureka, I have found it! 'Kindergarten' is the word." Thus he came upon the name accidentally. But, in his day to name the institution a "garden" was an audacious idea. The most modern kindergarten aims to be much more than a garden, a refuge or a nursery, though it has these values incidentally. The kindergarten aims to make use of the natural instinct of the child for play and to divert this activity into more orderly and meaningful channels than it would follow if left undirected. It aims to put before him certain ideals which he shall later make his own and which shall become effective motives in his post-kindergarten days. It aims, too, to create for the child a social environment which shall evoke his appreciation of a cultural social atmosphere. In the kindergarten he is more than 'Ego'. He is to realize that, however fondly his mother may regard him as the only important human unit, he is, as a matter of fact, but a single member of a large social group. In this way his thought and his interest become less self-centered and he learns something of the social arts and graces. It is from this point of view that the definition of the modern kindergarten is as given by Professor Monroe, "a society of children engaged in play and in various forms of self-expression, through which

the children learn something of the values and methods of social life without as yet being burdened by its
technique.''* But, in reality, it seems to me that some
kindergarteners are not well prepared to realize their
ideals. Perhaps because the followers of Froebel have
been chiefly women his theory and practice have been
carefully and faithfully 'conserved and cultivated
and there has not been, as yet, much reformation and
modification, especially in the play program. The
games, gifts and occupations are overemphasized and
in some kindergartens the outdoor-work has been al-
most eliminated. In any event, it seems to me that
there is much room for controversy in the methods of
the kindergarten training. These methods are not
limited to the kindergartens in Japan: this criticism
can also apply to some kindergartens in the United
States. When I was an instructor of education in a
Girls' Normal School in Japan I was asked by many
parents whether or not for a child there was any advantage in kindergarten training. Since then, the
kindergarten problem has been of particular interest
to me. I have sought to study the status of the kindergarten in different countries and more particularly
in Japan. The present thesis embodies the results
of this study.

*See Cyclopedia of Education, page 598.

CHAPTER II

A. Germany

PRACTICALLY no attention is given to infant education in the school systems of Germany. This nation which gave the world the discoverer of the kindergarten has never indorsed his ideas in any whole-hearted manner. Froebel established his first kindergarten at Blankenburg in 1837 (he named it Kindergarten in 1840;) but so little favor did it meet that between the years 1851 and 1861, it was officially prohibited in Prussia, and even to-day it has not been incorporated in the public school system of that kingdom.

Even the private kindergartens are not largely attended. The number of these private kindergartens is between 200 and 300.

B. Austria-Hungary

In Austria-Hungary infant schools had been organized before the kindergarten was invented, but the influence of Froebel began to be felt even during his life time, and the transformation of the infant schools was gradually effected. In 1872 kindergartens were made a part of the school system, and since then all

* Annual report of National Kindergarten Association (1911) pp. 23.

children between the ages of four and six have been compelled to attend either the kindergarten or the infant schools. Every normal school student is required to understand the educational principles of Froebel's kindergarten. In 1903 there were 77,000 children between the ages of three and six in the kindergartens of Austria, and 154,000 in those of Hungary. There was also a completely organized system of day nurseries, which enrolled 152,000 children. The kindergartens of Hungary compare well with the best in Switzerland and in the United States.

C. Switzerland

The first kindergarten in Switzerland was opened in 1872 in Zurich. In 1881 a national kindergarten association was organized there. In 1900 there were 767 kindergartens attended by 30,344 children between the ages of four and six.

D. The Netherlands

The kindergarten movement in the Netherlands was inspired by Baroness Marenholtz Von Bülow in 1858. In 1900 there were in that country 1,047 kindergartens and now there are both public and private kindergartens with a total of about 125,000 children.

E. Belgium

Kindergartens have existed here since 1842. In 1857 Baroness Von Bülow gave many lectures about

the kindergarten. In 1899 there were 2198 kindergartens and 222,068 children between three and six
were enrolled in these schools. Now more than 250,-
000 children are trained in the kindergartens.

F. Portugal

Infant schools of the 'maternal' or nursery type
enroll children from three to six years of age.

G. Russia

There are a few kindergartens here, some dating
back a quarter of a century.

H. Sweden

Infant education in Sweden is of the 'maternal'
rather than kindergarten type. There are over 5,000
infant schools, called *Smaskolar,* which prepare for
the elementary grades.

I. Australia

In this country infant schools, with a two-years'
course, are found in New South Wales and in Western
Australia.

J. Italy

In Italy the first kindergarten was opened in 1850.
Baroness Von Bülow lectured on the kindergarten
during 1871 to 1872 and at the end of the year her lec-

tures were published. Inspired by her, the Italians
founded a large kindergarten in Naples, and a few in
Florence, Rome and Venice. In 1907-8 there were
3,576 schools and 343,563 children who were being
trained in the kindergartens. As in other countries,
these institutions are private and communal, although
they receive grants from the general government.
They have been established in at least one-fourth of
the communes. Here in Italy, so called kindergartens
are in reality day nurseries, since children are allowed
to enter at the age of two and a half years. In Italy,
as in Japan, the lack of trained kindergarteners is a
source of weakness. Yet there are some very good
training courses in the normal schools, and excellent
private training schools in Naples, Verona, and Rome.
The Royal Froebel Institute, at Rome, received an
endowment from Victor Emmanuel II. Since 1907
Dr. Montessori has organized the infant school called
the *Casa dei Bambini*, or ''The Children's House'',
in Rome.

The essentials of her system are a strong emphasis
on sense training and great stress on the freedom of
the child. For the sense training there are many different pieces of apparatus designed to develop the several senses. As she was a close student of Itard and
Séguin, there are various wooden insets similar to
those used by them. The child learns to recognize the
form by passing the fingers around the edges of the
insets and then putting them in their proper places.
She also uses blocks of various sizes and silk bobbins

of different colors and shades, and letters cut from sandpaper. In addition to this somewhat formal sense training, there is buttoning and lacing cloth or leather fastened on frames. There is nothing new in this, however, as there have been many American schools which have used these methods in the training of feeble minded children for some time past. The second essential feature of the Montessori method is the freedom of the child. This principle, too, is not a new invention after all, as every student of educational history knows. Her distinguished service is rather the awakening of infant educators who have been tired of the repetition of the Froebel's gifts and occupations.

K. England

In 1854 Von Marenholtz Bülow visited England. There had already been established in London a Froebelian kindergarten, which was conducted by Mr. and Mrs. Ronge. In the same year there was an educational exhibition in the city.* To this exhibition Baroness Bülow presented the series of gifts and Mrs. Ronge gave a lecture on the exhibition. In fact, this was the first lecture about the kindergarten in England. This lecture awakened the prominent educators who were amazed at the new idea in pedagogy.

Then Madam Bülow published a book in English entitled, "Educational Mission of Women". Mr. Dickens also published an article in his "Household

*"Infant Schools" by David Salmon, pp. 116-122.

Words''* and wrote an explanatory essay on her book. By means of this book many English educators and society women were suddenly inspired and much interest was aroused.

In 1857 Miss Doreck came over from Wurtenberg and founded the London Kindergarten. Since 1861 Miss Eleonore Heerwart (who had been trained by Middendorff at Keilhau) and the Baroness Adèle de Portugal and Madame Emilie Michaelis came to England and these contributed much to the kindergarten movement.

For the first twenty years the effect of the propaganda was felt mainly in the private schools for the wealthy, though it had been commended by one of the inspectors of the eductional department as early as 1854. At length the London School Board was established in 1870 to investigate the conditions of the old schools and the new scheme. In February, 1871, a committee was appointed (with Professor Huxley as its chairman) to consider the curriculum to be adopted in the elementary schools.

In 1874 the Board appointed Miss Bishop to lecture on the kindergarten and in the same year the Croydon School Board appointed Madame Michaelis.

In the same year also the British and Foreign Training School established a kindergarten in connection with its college at Stockwell and invited Miss Heerwart to take charge of it. Thenceforth the germ of the kindergarten took quick root, and within a few

*No. 278, July 21st, 1855

[20]

years most Infant Schools regularly employed Froebel's games and many were imbued with his spirit. At present England is the foremost nation in the world in the provisions for educational facilities in the preliminary grade. Over 2,000,000 children between the ages of three and seven are enrolled in the English Infant Schools. Yet, strictly speaking, these schools are not real kindergartens, but ordinary schools for teaching the rudiments, with some kindergarten attachments. They lead directly into the elementary school.

L. France

France, like England, retained the Infant Schools (though they call them the Maternal Schools, *écoles maternelles*) instead of adopting the kindergarten. The Baroness Von Bülow's efforts in France in 1855 resulted in many reforms in the maternal schools of the country; although, as a result of the feeling aroused by the French-Prussian war, everything German, even the name Kindergarten, was rejected, and progress in that line came to an end.

The *écoles maternelles* and the *classes enfantines* do not follow the teaching of Froebel, but exist chiefly for social and economic reasons. They are primarily designed in the interest of the mothers whose household or business duties demand all their time. These schools relieve them of the care of their young children. The hours at school are long, frequently from

[21]

7 A. M. to 7 P. M., and there is much work and little play. The teachers are women, most of whom are not specially trained. In 1906-1907 the *Écoles Maternelles* enrolled 651,955 children between the ages of two and six years.

M.   United States

In the United States the kindergarten has been cordially received. Its principles have influenced the public school system and have in turn been developed and modified by it. And here we can find the best kindergartens and the best organization of the institution in the world.

The development of the kindergarten movement in the United States may be traced by the following dates:

1827. An Infant School Society was formed in New York City in the interest of children from three to six years of age, but it was incorporated into the New York Public Society.

1855. Mrs. Carl Schurz, who had studied under Froebel, established at Watertown, Wisconsin, the first American Kindergarten. All the early kindergartens were conducted by the cultured German immigrants and German was spoken in them.

1860. The first ardent American apostle of the kindergarten, Miss Elizabeth Peabody opened a kindergarten in Boston. She was the sister-in-law of Horace Mann.

1868. The first American school for training kindergarten teachers was opened in Boston.

1872. Miss Maria Bölte opened a training school in New York.

1873. Another training school was established in New York. Both schools were conducted by ladies who had been trained under Froebel's associates in Europe.

1873. The first public kindergarten was opened by the School Board of St. Louis, Mo., under the superintendency of Dr. Harris. It was conducted by Miss Susan E. Blow and with such success as to establish it firmly in the St. Louis system and to encourage similar experiments in other cities.

1876-1889. Mrs. Quincy A. Shaw supported the entire free kindergarten system of Boston.

1881. The kindergarten was adopted as part of its public school system at Milwaukee, Wisconsin.

The following cities also adopted the kindergarten as part of their school system in these early years.

1883.	Des Moines, Ia.	1891.	Lexington, Ky.
1884.	Portland, Me.	1891.	Utica, N. Y.
1886.	New Orleans, La.	1892.	St. Paul, Minn.
1886.	Hartford, Conn.	1893.	Chicago, Ill.
1887.	Philadelphia, Pa.	1893.	Worcester, Mass.
1888.	Rochester, N. Y.	1893.	New York, N. Y.
1889.	Los Angeles, Cal.	1893.	Omaha, Neb.

The general idea of the growth of the kindergartens in the United States will be indicated from the following data:

In 1902 there were in the United States a total of 3,244 kindergartens, with an enrollment of 205,432 children. The census of 1900 gave a population of 3,636,583 children between 4 and 6 years of age, so that a little more than 5% of the children between the ages of 4 and 6 were receiving kindergarten training in 1902. Ten years later we find 7,557 kindergartens with an enrollment of 353,546 children. The census of 1910 gives a population of 4,150,815 children between 4 and 6 years of age. In 1912, therefore, approximately 9% of the children of kindergarten age were in the kindergartens.*

Figure 1 (Bulletin 1914 No. 6 pp. 15.) shows the numbers of children enrolled in kindergarten per 1000 of the population between 4 and 6 years of age in 1912.

N. Summary

The foregoing figures indicate the development of the Kindergarten externally. This sort of measurement, however, "is akin to standing a little child against the kitchen door and measuring its height every six months, and letting it triumphantly view the new scratch which shows how it is 'growing!' But no series of ascending scratches can record the development of the little child's mind and power."** Now, let me describe its development from within. It seems to me that the only real Froebelian Kindergartens are to be found in the United States. In Germany we are not able to find them, though Germany gave

*U. S. Bulletin, 1914, No. 6. "Kindergarten in the United States" pp. 7.
**U. S. Bulletin, 1914, No. 6., pp. 7.

FIG. I

Number of children enrolled in kindergartens per thousand of the population between 4 and 6 years of age in 1912.

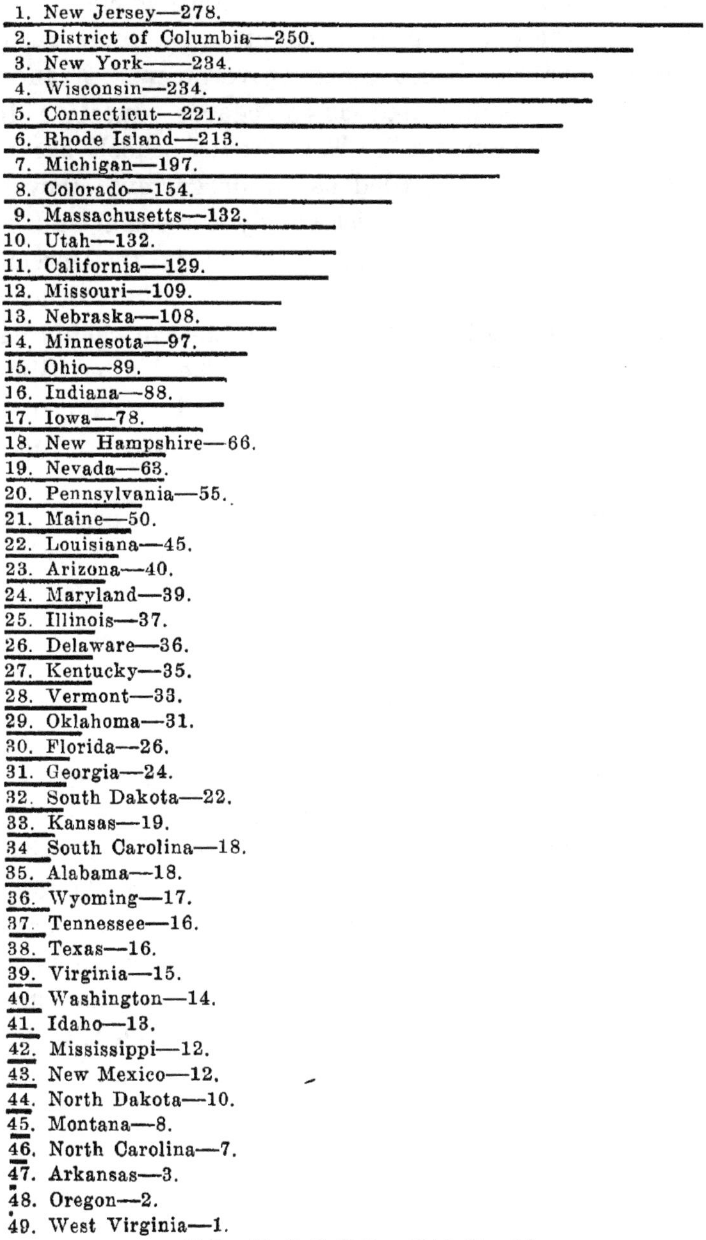

1. New Jersey—278.
2. District of Columbia—250.
3. New York——234.
4. Wisconsin—234.
5. Connecticut—221.
6. Rhode Island—213.
7. Michigan—197.
8. Colorado—154.
9. Massachusetts—132.
10. Utah—132.
11. California—129.
12. Missouri—109.
13. Nebraska—108.
14. Minnesota—97.
15. Ohio—89.
16. Indiana—88.
17. Iowa—78.
18. New Hampshire—66.
19. Nevada—63.
20. Pennsylvania—55.
21. Maine—50.
22. Louisiana—45.
23. Arizona—40.
24. Maryland—39.
25. Illinois—37.
26. Delaware—36.
27. Kentucky—35.
28. Vermont—33.
29. Oklahoma—31.
30. Florida—26.
31. Georgia—24.
32. South Dakota—22.
33. Kansas—19.
34. South Carolina—18.
35. Alabama—18.
36. Wyoming—17.
37. Tennessee—16.
38. Texas—16.
39. Virginia—15.
40. Washington—14.
41. Idaho—13.
42. Mississippi—12.
43. New Mexico—12.
44. North Dakota—10.
45. Montana—8.
46. North Carolina—7.
47. Arkansas—3.
48. Oregon—2.
49. West Virginia—1.

(After U. S. Bulletin, 1914, No. 6.)

to the world the founder of the kindergarten. Even to-day there are in that country no kindergartens which are established by the government. France is one of the leading nations as regards education during the "tender age". The French schools are not, however, to be regarded as Kindergartens; they are really nurseries and exist chiefly for social and economical reasons. Again, England is the foremost nation in infant education, yet her "Infant Schools" are ordinary schools for teaching the rudiments with some kindergarten attachments. The United States, on the other hand, has adopted and developed the kindergarten more thoroughly than any European country.

Opened by cultured German immigrants, inspired by the so-called "ardent American apostle of the Kindergarten", Miss Peabody of Boston, the kindergarten started its career in America. It was introduced into the public school system by William T. Harris and W. N. Hailmann.

In the St. Louis Kindergarten, Miss Susan Blow emphasized symbolism and industrial training. And she has been the prominent leader of the conservative school. She advocated a close adherence to Froebel's fundamental educational principles. On the other hand, there are at present many prominent leaders of the younger progressive school. They believe in the selection of materials, games, miniature industrial processes, etc., from the world with which the child comes into daily contact, as a means of aiding him

[26]

to appreciate this world instead of adhering to those materials which Froebel selected from the relatively primitive village life in Blankenburg, Keilhau and other places with which he was associated. The progressives also, as a rule, do not emphasize the symbolic values which inhere in Froebel's devices. They are supported by modern psychologists' analysis of child experiences, represented by Professor John Dewey. As a partial explanation of Froebel's belief in symbolism, Dewey presents this very suggestive critique of our own Kindergartens:

"It must be remembered that much of Froebel's symbolism is the product of two peculiar conditions of his own life and work. In the first place, on account of inadequate knowledge at that time of the physiological and psychological facts and principles of a child's growth, he was often forced to resort to a strained and artificial explanation of the value attaching to play, etc. To the impartial observer it is obvious that many of his statements are cumbrous and far-fetched, giving abstract philosophical reasoning for matters that now receive a simple every-day formulation. In the second place, the general political and social conditions of Germany were such that it was impossible to conceive continuity between the free co-operative life of the kindergarten and that of the (reactionary monarchical) world outside. Accordingly he could not regard the occupations of the schoolroom as literal reproductions of the ethical principles involved in community life,—the latter were often too restricted and authoritative to serve as worthy models. Accordingly, he was compelled to think of them as symbolic of abstract ethical and philosophical principles. There certainly is change enough and progress enough in the social conditions of the United States of to-day, as compared with those of Germany of his day, to justify making kindergarten activities more natural, more direct, and more real representations of current life than Froebel's disciples have done.''*

E. L. Thorndike more emphatically concludes after giving many examples, '' . . . No one has ever given a particle of valid evidence to show any such preposterous associations in children's minds between plain things and these far-away abstractions.''**

Thus, the psychological tendency of the progressive kindergarteners in the United States is to emphasize reality rather than Froebelian symbolism. Especially, the experiment made in Dewey's reconstructed kindergarten marked a real epoch in kindergarten training. There is no doubt that the Montessori method has also made some contribution (as I have stated before) to the American kindergarten.***

The first comparative investigation of sixteen thousand eighth grade graduates of the public schools of New York City, made by Dr. Leonard P. Ayres in

*Elementary School Record 1900, p. 145.
**''Notes on Child Study'' by E. L. Thorndike, 1908, p. 80.
***See U. S. Bulletin 1914, No. 28, ''The Montessori Method and the Kindergarten.''

1909, to which reference will be made later in the thesis, raised some doubts as to the efficiency of the kindergarten in that City. The kindergarten Association is also active in studying various aspects of kindergarten and non-kindergarten pupils in the United States.

This critical attitude toward the Froebelian kindergarten is also reflected in several investigations made to determine the work of the kindergarten by studying its effects on the children attending it. All in all, the future of the American Kindergarten is promising.

CHAPTER III

THE KINDERGARTEN IN JAPAN

A. *Its Development and Present Status*

IN my own country the first kindergarten was opened November 14th, 1876, in connection with the Girls' Higher Normal School in Tokyo. It was just 36 years after the opening of Froebel's kindergarten in Blankenburg. The kindergarten was attended by children between three and six years of age. The first enrollment was 158 children. In most other countries the first kindergarten was private, but in Japan the first one was a government kindergarten. In a few years, there were many public and private kindergartens.

In 1881, kindergartens increased to 17 in number with 1116 children; in 1890 there were 138 kindergartens; in 1900, 241. In 1889 a Kindergarten and Training Shool were organized in Kobe Girls' College, under the leadership of Miss Annie L. Howe. This institution has been one of the important centers for the training of kindergarten teachers. In 1910 there were 443 kindergartens, 1,253 teachers and 37,298 children, while there were 6,795,809 elementary school pupils. Thus, in 1910 about 6% of the elementary school pupils were receiving kindergarten training.

B. The Object of the First Kindergarten in Tokyo

We find the object of the first Kindergarten in the following sentence: "It receives children three to six years of age, exercises their natural senses, develops the waking mind, strengthens their bodies, cultivates their emotion and trains to politeness in language and conduct (1876)."*

C. The Training of Kindergarteners in Japan

There have been two centers for the training of kindergarten teachers. One is the government institution in Tokyo; the other, which is in Kobe, is supervised by the American Missionary. These training schools are not sufficient for the need of the kindergarten teachers. So, even now, it is common to find only one trained teacher and two or three untrained teachers in the Kindergarten.

In general, we have adopted the training methods of American Kindergartens. The Tokyo kindergarten is trying to modify the method, so as to fit it for the country's children, considering the customs and manners.

D. The Laws Concerning the Kindergartens

In 1899, a regulation limited the number of infants per teacher to forty and the total number of the kindergarten children in each school to one hundred,

"Encyclopaedia Japonica" 1908, pp. 1570.

though under special conditions there may be enrolled one hundred and fifty children.

In 1911 the regulation was changed so that a kindergarten would enroll 120, and under special conditions 200 children.

The following rules were fixed in 1899 for the equipment of the kindergarten.

I. The building must have one story and must be equipped with nursing room, play-room, teacher's room and the other necessary rooms.

II. The area of the nursing room must be more than one *tsubo* (about 4 sq. yards) for four children.

III. It must be equipped with gifts, pictures, play-materials, musical instruments, blackboard, desks, benches, chairs, clock, thermometer, stoves and other necessary things.

IV. It is customary to make the area of the play-ground 1 tsubo per child.

V. The school site, drinking water and lighting must follow the rules for the elementary school.

For a time there was a tendency to think of the kindergarten as a preparatory school for the elementary school. Teachers taught the same materials as were taught in the elementary school in their attempt to carry out this idea. Observing this tendency, the government warned the teachers. In Act 196 of the Imperial Ordinance on Elementary Schools we find the following rules:

I. Infant training should supplement home education by cultivating a sound mind and good habits.

II. Infant training must be in harmony with the degree of the development of the child's mind and body. It is prohibited to teach him material which is hard to understand or to do.

III. In education teachers must pay attention to the child's individuality and always try to get him to imitate the teacher's good manners.

E. The Old Curriculum

The curriculum in 1899 was as follows:

I. PLAY.

    a. Voluntary play.
    b. Co-operative play.

In the play children practice the various activities with music to make them cheerful and to develop sound bodies.

II. MUSIC.

This serves to train the auditory, vocal and respiratory organs and to make children cheerful.

III. STORIES.

The stories must be useful and interesting. The materials are allegories, fables and stories about natural and manufactured objects. The stories ought to train the child in the use of accurate language, to cultivate the virtues and to train the capacity for observation and attention.

[34]

IV. OCCUPATIONS.

These will attempt to train the pupil's hands and eyes and to cultivate his mind by the use of the kindergarten "gifts."

F. Present Principles in the Kindergarten Training

I. OBSERVATION.

Observation is to train the senses, to increase the child's ideas of objects and to cultivate his ability to observe things and to be attentive.

II. CONVERSATION.

a. *Listening.*

The teacher tells useful and interesting stories for the pupils to hear. Thus, the auditory sense is trained and also the mind.

b. *Dialogue.*

The teacher and children talk with each other and train their speech organs.

1. The materials of the conversation must be the common stories of Japan.

2. In the stories it is better to use pictures, wherever possible.

3. Repeat the same story many times.

4. The teacher's pronunciation must be plain and clear.

5. It is wise to let the children talk when they know something of the subject.

[35]

6. Let them listen to the teacher's whispering and so train their auditory senses.

III. MUSIC.

a. Songs must be simple and easy to understand.

b. The content of the song must be the common daily phenomena of children's experiences which will interest them.

c. Music must range between D and d. The time may be 4/4 or 2/4.

d. It is preferable to teach them music which is cheerful and suitable for marching.

e. In order to stimulate understanding and interest let them accompany songs with gestures.

f. The teacher's voice serves better as a guide to the child than do instruments.

IV. OCCUPATION.

Occupation by use of toys trains the hands and eyes, and develops the mind and body.

a. Arrangement.
b. Blocks (the fifth gift).
c. Ball.
d. Top, (wooden top plays on the desk).
e. Otetama, (small bean bags).
f. Ohajiki, etc. (a sort of carom).

[36]

V. MANUAL TRAINING.

Through simple productions the Kindergarten trains the hands and eyes, cultivates the mental abilities of originality, imagination, and æsthetic feeling and trains directly for sustained effort in work.

    a. Bean work (constructive work with soaked beans and small bamboo sticks).
    b. Modeling.
    c. Paper folding.
    d. Needle work or embroidery.
    e. Other gifts, etc.

VI. DRAWING.

Teachers ought to develop well the pupil's ability to express his ideas in pictures and at the same time train his hands and eyes, and cultivate æsthetic feelings. Teachers must be aware of the following points:

    a. The teacher ought to show some simple pictures drawn in order to interest them.

    b. Let children practice accurate arm movement.

VII. PLAY AND METHOD OF GUIDING IT.

    A. *Their classification of play is thus:*
Social or Co-operative Play.

    1. March.
    2. Simple Games.

[37]

3. Imitative Exercises.

Individual or Special Play.
1. Imitative Plays.
2. Gardening.
3. Collecting (plants, insects, pebbles, etc.).
4. Kikai play (play of swing, wagon, rope, etc.).

B. Leading principles of play for the teachers.*

a. Do not force children to participate in so-called kindergarten play from the very beginning. Guide their play instincts naturally.

b. Teachers ought to study the development of the play instincts.
1. Play must be intuitive at first.
2. The imitative stage comes next.
3. Then comes the expressive stage.

c. Kindergarten play should consist of real play, amusement, a little art and work, but no labor or drudgery.

d. The real value of play is in concentration or forgetting everything outside. Harm may be done if the teacher disturbs this concentration by seeking to adhere too much to the rules for the sake of formal appearances.

*We can say that the original discoverer of the importance of play in education was Plato; its rediscoverer was Froebel; and its reconstructor is John Dewey. Kindergarten teachers ought to study the theory and practice of play. Japanese Kindergarten teachers are not yet acquainted with Dewey's suggestions, although much attention is paid to play and its guidance.

e. The teacher should be a kind supervisor, not a meddler.

f. The teacher ought to take advantage of the good opportunities to observe the individualities of the children during their play. It will help her to control them.

g. The teacher should herself take part in the play and she must not break the children's rules, even though she is their supervisor.

VIII. DISCIPLINE.

In Japan the government, as well as the school teachers, put much emphasis on moral instruction. Character building occupies the first place and receives first consideration in all training and education of the young. Physical training and book-learning take second and third place. Act I of the Imperial Ordinance on elementary schools shows the Japanese educator's attitude toward the training of the physical, mental, and moral traits:

"Elementary schools are designed to give children the rudiments of moral education and of civic education, together with such general knowledge and skill as are necessary for life, while due attention is paid to their bodily development."

There is in Japan much conscious dependence upon the school as the moulder of character. On this account kindergarten teachers are paying due attention to the discipline of the children. Of course, as to discipline, the teacher cannot teach by words alone but should teach as well by her own good manners and example. We cannot expect to train moral judgment directly, yet by careful supervision teachers can develop good habits and manners. They are, in fact, trying to teach the following manners:

a. Greeting each acquaintance on the way to kindergarten.
b. Wiping shoes at the entrance of the school and rooms.
c. Good posture.
d. Listening attitude.
e. Not to run in the classroom.
f. Keeping the schoolroom clean.
g. Taking care of toys and equipments.
h. Manners in the classroom.
i. Manners on the playground.
j. Table manners.
k. Cleaning finger nails.
l. Habit of helping themselves.
m. Salutation of parent on leaving and returning home. (This is the custom in Japan).
n. Obedience to parents.
o. Friendliness among brothers, sisters and playmates.
p. Honesty.
q. Courage, etc.

CHAPTER IV

THE EFFECT OF KINDERGARTEN TRAINING UPON THE PHYSICAL, MENTAL AND MORAL TRAITS OF JAPANESE SCHOOL CHILDREN

A. Object of the Investigation

THE object of the investigation was to secure general information in regard to certain traits of kindergarten children enumerated in the following question-naire. The result is of great importance to parents, to teachers of the kindergarten or elementary school, to supervisors and to school authorities. Some educators in Japan think that there is no need of kindergarten training for normal children if the mother can pay due attention to them. Others emphasize the need of transition classes. Some teachers praise blindly the effect of the training, while others are quite skeptical. I know also that in the United States some prominent educators believe that money devoted to kindergarten training is more than wasted. Yet, the number of the kindergartens is increasing year after year. The investigation of the effect of kindergarten training is not less important and it suggests many worthy queries.

a. If we should find by the use of still other and more comprehensive investigations that the effect of the kindergarten is inappreciable or positively harmful to the subsequent development of children, it would be wise to prohibit the establishment of kindergartens, as did a Prussian Prime Minister in the time of Froebel. If there be definite good effects, it will be well to know the example that California set: "Upon petition of parents or guardians of twenty-five or more children between the ages of four and a half and six, residing within a mile of an elementary school, and with the approval of the School Authorities, the Board of Education shall establish and maintain a kindergarten."* And if there be good effects we would recommend the establishing of kindergartens in our Japanese Girls' Schools and also of classes for training kindergarteners and future mothers.

b. If, again, it be found in the grades that some traits of kindergarten children are more desirable than those of nonkindergarten children, parents and elementary school teachers would get some hints for their training methods; on the other hand, if the traits of kindergarten children are less desirable than those of non-kindergarten children, the kindergarteners and their supervisors should know this and contrive some remedy for the difficulty. To know what group of traits is stronger or weaker than the other group is of no less interest.

c. The author does not pretend to solve all of these problems nor does he assume that any one study can settle conclusively these important questions. The data which follow, however, furnish a basis for answering some of these questions and give suggestions to all of them.

*Extract from recent enactment, furnished by the special committee of The International Kindergarten Union.

THE KINDERGARTEN IN JAPAN

B. Method of the Investigation

The data which are received in the article were secured by means of the questionnaire which is reproduced herewith. One thousand copies of it were distributed to 75 typical schools. Returns were received from 28 schools. The questionnaire was given to each teacher of each grade. They were asked to fill out all the blanks. But in order to save the teacher's time and also to get many returns, the author asked teachers (with the exception of those in Hiroshima City), to grade only kindergarten children in each of the eleven qualities. The grading was to be done as conscientiously as possible. The blanks under each trait were then to be filled out to show how many kindergarten children belong to the A, B, and C group in each class.

In Hiroshima City the author himself went to each school, saw the teachers, explained the grading method, answered the questions and studied the traits of *both* kindergarten children and nonkindergarten children. Taking the results which were obtained in Hiroshima as the standard, the author has tried to compare the results of the other groups.

The study includes, then, data from twenty-four elementary schools in nineteen cities (24 = 20 in 18 cities, and 4 in Hiroshima City) ; three Middle Schools in three cities and five girls' schools in five cities. The data from the Middle Schools and Girls' School have been used only for the sake of

[43]

comparison. The main effort has been expended upon
the data from the elementary schools and here the
material from 20 cities represents estimates upon the
kindergarten pupil only and that from Hiroshima,
upon both kindergarten and nonkindergarten pupils.

Hiroshima City was selected as the standard city,
because conditions there are favorable for such a
study. Thus: (1) Hiroshima is a city which has, in
its 200,000 population, comparatively few of the very
rich or very poor class; (2) the kindergartens have
been established there for over 20 years; (3) kindergarten training has been regarded favorably; (4)
there are many good elementary schools,—one is the
training school of Hiroshima Higher Normal School;
another, the Training School of a Model Normal
School, and the others are also of good quality; (5)
there is the tendency among the teachers to stay
longer in the same school than in other cities.

The teachers were also asked to set down in the
space left in the middle of the questionnaire their
general criticisms of the kindergarten children. From
these records, the author aimed to find the general
opinion of the teachers concerning the merits and
desirability of the kindergarten.

About the estimations of Japanese elementary
school teachers the author believes that they are comparatively reliable for these reasons: (1) in general,
they teach the same pupils for many years (some
teach the same pupils from the first grade up to their
graduation); (2) they try to study the individuality

[44]

	No. of pupils in each group A B C:
Attention 66	A B C
Patience	A B C
Decision	A B C
Understanding	A B C
Memory	A B C
Imagination	A B C
Friendliness	A B C
Love of natural object	A B C
Scholarship	A B C
Moral conduct	A B C
Health	A B C
Average age of kindergarten children	
Average age of the grade children	

Teacher's General Criticisms of the Kindergarten Children

(1)

(2)

(3)

(4)

Grading Standard

90 group (86-100) A
70 group (66-85) B
50 group (lower than 65) C

Those who are trained in the kindergarten within

1) 1 year are ( )
2) 2 years are ( )
3) 3 years are ( )

Physical, mental and moral traits of kindergarten children

[45]

of their pupils; (3) every school has the record of every pupil, concerning parentage, school career, school marks, physical traits, individuality, etc.

To save space in the tables and to avoid repetition, K. in this paper signifies Kindergarten children, NK. NonKindergarten.

In order to compare the K. and NK. pupils in each trait, it is evidently desirable to reduce their standing to a single standard. The author has reduced the values to percents by multiplying them by the quantity indicating their value; i. e., all A%'s have been multiplied by 9, all B%'s by 7, and all C%'s by 5 respectively, according to the grading standards. Thus, for example in Attention of Grade I, the author got 724, being the sum of $31 \times 9 + 50 \times 7 + 19 \times 5$.

Fig. II shows the result of this comparison, the nnn columns are the traits of NK. pupils of the common elementary schools in Hiroshima City, and kkk columns are those of K. pupils in the same schools.

Inspection of Fig. II shows that K. were judged superior in understanding, imagination, and scholarship; but judged in the other traits, distinctly inferior. These results were quite different from what had been expected.

Fig. III is the comparison of NK. of the common elementary schools in Hiroshima City and K. of twenty typical common elementary schools in 18 cities. Here it appears that in imagination and scholarship there was not as much difference between K. and NK. as in the former comparison, yet the traits in which

[46]

TABLE I

Percents of pupils graded A, B, and C in each trait of Kindergarten children in 20 Common elementary schools.

1. Attention
2. Patience
3. Decision
4. Understanding
5. Memory
6. Imagination
7. Friendliness
8. Love of natural objects
9. Scholarship
10. Moral conduct
11. Health

	Total No.	No. K.	1			2			3			4		
			A	B	C	A	B	C	A	B	C	A	B	C
I Grade	1420	449	31	50	19	25	59	16	24	60	16	37	51	12
II Grade	1547	382	34	46	20	27	53	20	28	55	17	42	43	15
III Grade	1532	385	33	43	24	27	53	20	29	50	21	41	42	17
IV Grade	1310	316	39	42	19	36	47	17	36	43	21	40	42	18
V Grade	1311	316	33	45	22	35	42	23	31	46	23	31	46	23
VI Grade	992	271	38	44	18	33	52	15	37	48	15	40	41	19
Average			35	45	20	30	51	19	30	51	19	40	43	17
VII and VIII	215	73	32	42	26	27	48	25	29	44	27	33	38	29
Middle School	1753	341	21	64	15	15	73	12	20	69	11	26	60	14
Girls' School	2427	348	28	55	17	23	61	16	19	65	16	27	52	21
Average			27	51	19	22	61	17	23	59	18	28	50	22
Whole Average			31	49	20	26	56	18	27	55	18	34	47	19

5			6			7			8			9			10			11		
A	B	C	A	B	C	A	B	C	A	B	C	A	B	C	A	B	C	A	B	C
39	45	16	34	54	12	35	56	9	31	62	7	38	47	15	31	57	12	54	41	5
39	47	14	33	53	13	32	58	10	34	58	8	42	46	12	35	51	14	42	49	9
37	47	16	31	54	15	33	56	11	36	55	9	38	44	18	33	53	14	38	56	6
42	42	16	38	49	13	36	53	11	40	51	9	37	49	14	38	51	11	50	44	6
42	38	20	40	43	17	39	45	16	43	42	15	41	43	16	36	54	10	43	50	7
41	44	15	32	58	10	40	46	14	32	58	10	41	44	15	39	50	11	50	41	9
40	44	16	35	52	13	36	52	12	36	34	10	40	46	14	35	53	12	46	47	7
36	38	26	38	38	24	26	60	14	27	54	19	30	53	17	30	70	0	47	45	8
26	61	13	17	70	13	22	75	3	32	60	8	25	53	22	21	67	12	37	57	6
29	56	15	25	60	15	29	63	8	33	64	3	29	48	23	19	77	4	47	48	5
30	52	18	27	56	17	26	66	8	31	59	10	28	51	21	23	71	6	44	50	6
35	48	17	22	54	15	31	59	10	34	56	10	34	48	18	29	62	9	45	48	7

[47]

FIG. II

The nnn columns are the traits of non-Kg. children of the common elementary schools in Hiroshima City

The kkk columns are the traits of Kg. children of the common elementary schools in Hiroshima City

1 Attention
2 Patience
3 Decision
4 Understanding
5 Memory
6 Imagination
7 Friendliness
8 Love of natural objects
9 Scholarship
10 Moral conduct
11 Health

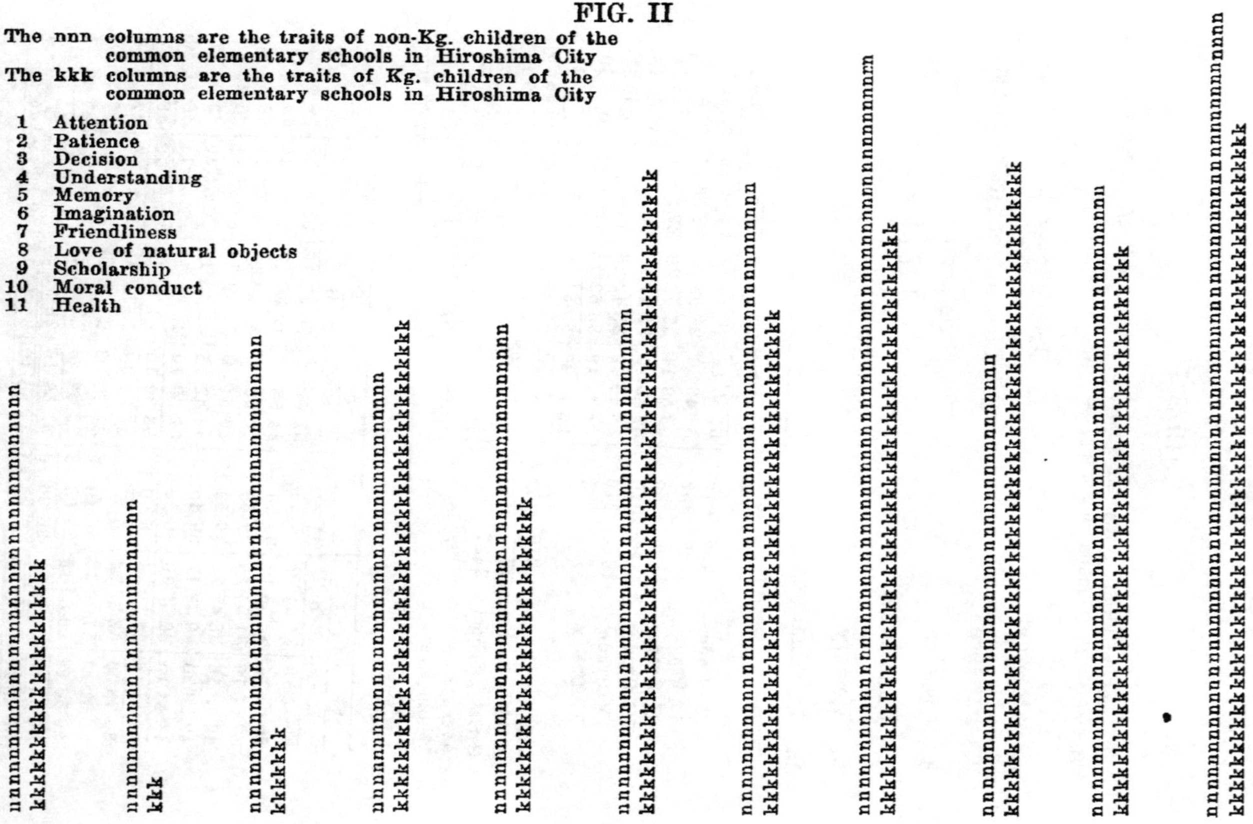

[48]

FIG. III

The nnnn columns are the traits of non-Kg. children of the
common elementary schools in Hiroshima City
The kkkk columns are the traits of kindergarten children of the
20 typical common elementary schools in Japan

1 Attention
2 Patience
3 Decision
4 Understanding
5 Memory
6 Imagination
7 Friendliness
8 Love of natural objects
9 Scholarship
10 Moral conduct
11 Health

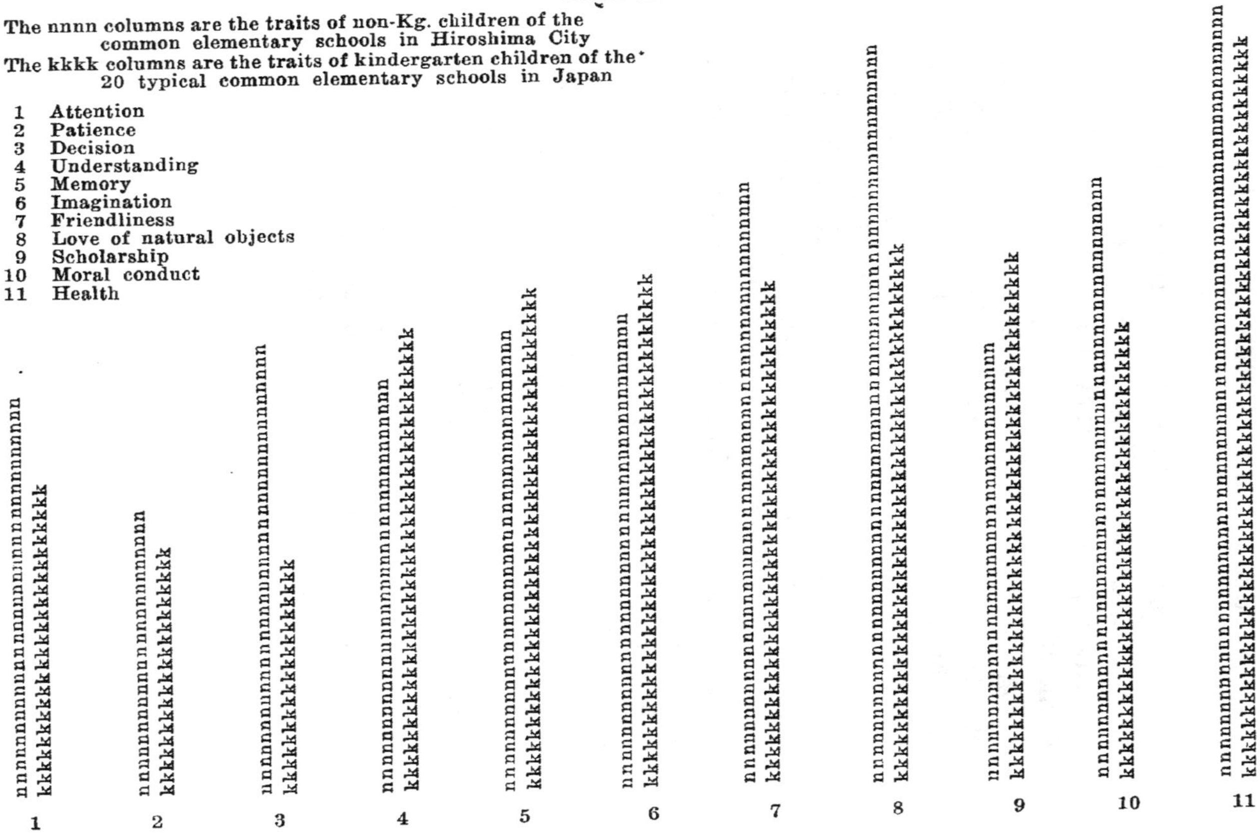

[49]

the K. were superior to the NK. were exactly the same ones, *i. e.*, understanding, imagination, memory and scholarship: and again they were inferior to the NK. in the other traits.

Fig. IV shows the combined comparison of the five groups. The aaa columns are the traits of NK. of common elementary schools in Hiroshima City, the bbb columns are those of K. of 20 typical common elementary schools in 18 cities, the ccc columns are those of K. of common elementary schools in Hiroshima City, the ddd columns are those NK. of higher elementary schools in Hiroshima City, and the eee columns are those of 20 higher elementary schools in 18 cities.

Fig. V is the comparison of three groups of common elementary schools. In this case the K. groups surpass in understanding, memory, imagination and scholarship as mentioned before.

Fig. VI is the comparison of pupils who were attending the higher elementary schools. Here, K. were superior in imagination and scholarship but inferior in other traits. The reader must understand in this case that there is a general tendency for the superior pupils to enter the Middle Schools, Girls' Schools and the Normal Schools.

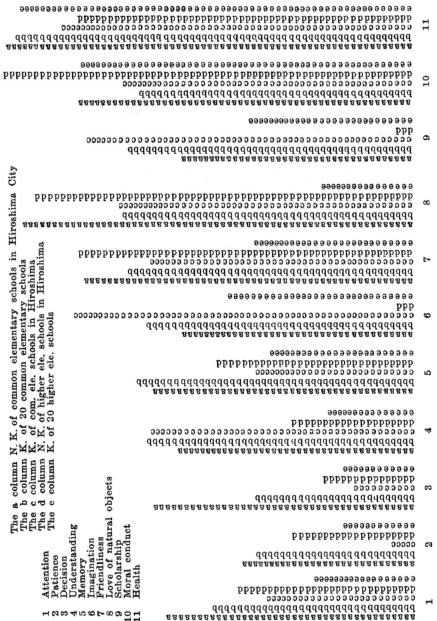

FIG. IV

The a column N. K. of common elementary schools in Hiroshima City
The b column K. of 20 common elementary schools
The c column K. of com. ele. schools in Hiroshima
The d column N. K. of higher ele. schools in Hiroshima
The e column K. of 20 higher ele. schools

1 Attention
2 Patience
3 Decision
4 Understanding
5 Memory
6 Imagination
7 Friendliness
8 Love of natural objects
9 Scholarship
10 Moral conduct
11 Health

FIG. V

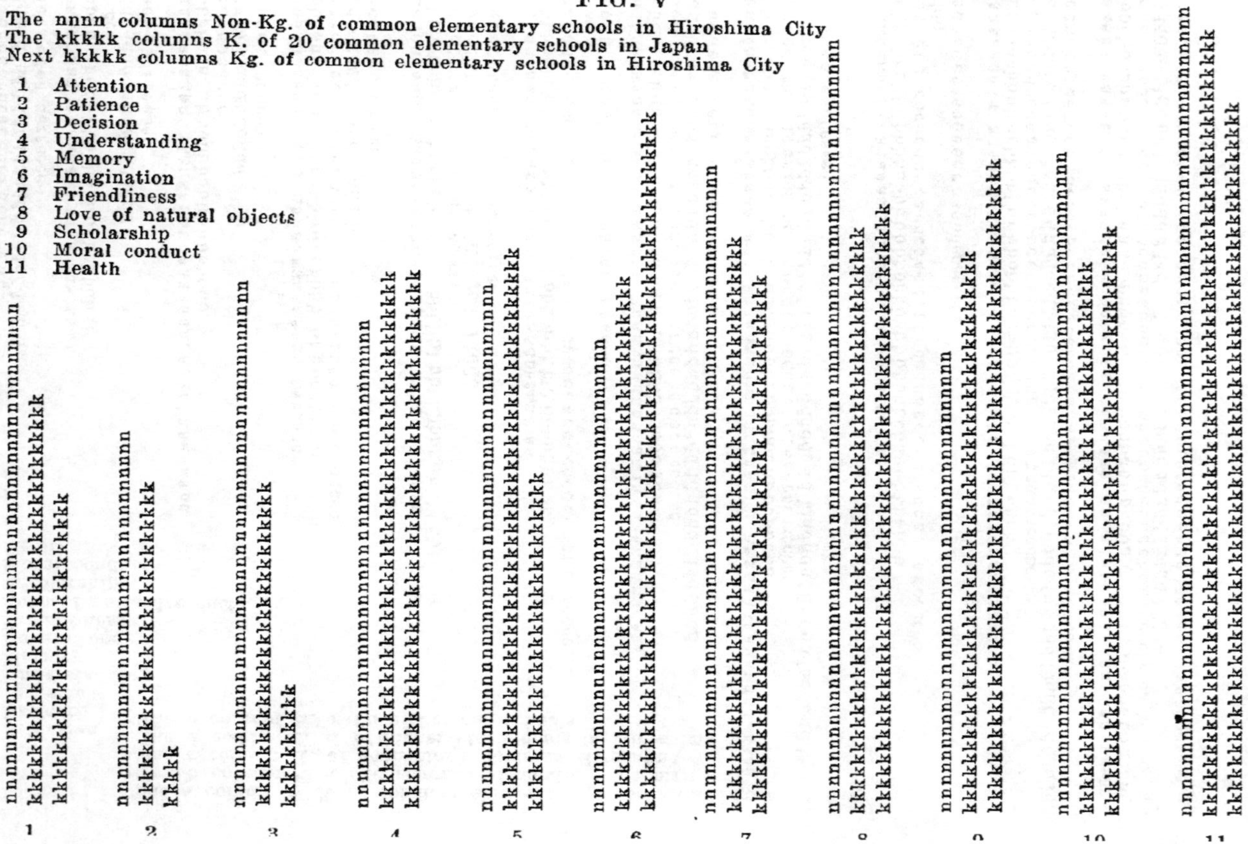
The nnnn columns Non-Kg. of common elementary schools in Hiroshima City
The kkkkk columns K. of 20 common elementary schools in Japan
Next kkkkk columns Kg. of common elementary schools in Hiroshima City
1 Attention
2 Patience
3 Decision
4 Understanding
5 Memory
6 Imagination
7 Friendliness
8 Love of natural objects
9 Scholarship
10 Moral conduct
11 Health
1
2
3
4
5
6
7
8
9
10
11

Attention

1 Attention
2 Patience
3 Decision
4 Understanding
5 Memory
6 Imagination
7 Friendliness
8 Love of natural objects
9 Scholarship
10 Moral conduct
11 Health

[53]

FIG. VII

Non-Kg. of common elementary schools in Hiroshima City
nnnnnnnnnnnnnnnnnnnnnnnnnnnnnnnnnnnnnnnnnnnnnnnnnnn
Total sum 8250.   Average 750.

Kg. of 20 common elementary schools in 18 cities
kkkkkkkkkkkkkkkkkkkkkkkkkkkkkkkkkkkkkkkkkkkkk
Total sum 8188.   Average 744.

Kg. of common elementary schools in Hiroshima City
kkkkkkkkkkkkkkkkkkkkkkkkkkkkkkkkkkkkkkkkk
Total sum 8127.   Average 738.

Non-Kg. of higher elementary schools in Hiroshima City
nnnnnnnnnnnnnnnnnnnnnnnnnnnnnnnnnnnn
Total sum 8045.   Average 731.

Kg. students of 5 Girls' schools
kkkkkkkkkkkkkkkkkkkkkkkkkkkkkkkkk
Total sum 8042.   Average 731.

Kg. of 20 higher elementary schools
kkkkkkkkkkkkkkkkkkkkkkkkkkk
Total sum 7981.   Average 725.

Kg. students of 3 Middle schools
kkkkkkkkkkkkkkkkkkkkkkkkkkk
Total sum 7967.   Average 724.

Fig. VII shows the comparison of the total number of each trait of each group and their averages. The higher column signifies that the teachers estimated the group better than others. The inspection of the figure tells us distinctly that NK. come first in common elementary schools, and also NK. surpasses K. in higher elementary schools. About the Middle Schools and the Girls' Schools the author cannot say anything of the comparison of K. and NK.

In order to investigate whether or not there is any correlation between these groups, the author tried to find co-efficients of correlation between both K. groups or both NK. groups, etc. For this purpose, the author used Spearman's rank-order method. For illustration the author will describe the case of the series of traits of K. in 20 common elementary schools (K. 20 C. E. S.) and those of K. in common elementary schools in Hiroshima City (K. C. E. S. H.).

The author found that there was the highest correlation (83) between the traits of the K of 20 common elementary schools and those of K. of common elementary schools in Hiroshima. Its P. E. was .09. There was the least correlation between K. of 20 common elementary schools and NK. of Higher elementary schools in Hiroshima City. From these investigations the author can assume that between both K. groups there is higher correlation than between K. and NK. groups. Further inference from these data the author leaves to the readers.

C. The Classification of the Teachers' Criticisms of the Kindergarten Children

The total number of the criticisms offered by teachers in the grade schools was 269. The following classification will bring out the chief features:

THE KINDERGARTEN IN JAPAN

TABLE II

INTELLECTUAL SIDE (62)

Strong Points		WEAK POINTS	
1 Better scholarship	18	1 Superficial knowledge ...	3
2 Better marks in manual training	12	2 Bad scholarship	3
3 Better expression	7		
4 Well developed reasoning power	6		
5 Developed imagination ..	5		
6 In general, their intellectual development is better than in the other group	5		
7 Know the day's news better than the other group	3		
Total	56	Total	6

EMOTIONAL SIDE (43)

1 Sympathy	9	1 They become too familiar in bad sense	4
2 Social attitude	8	2 Too capricious	4
3 Humor	5	3 Weep easily	3
4 Love of natural objects..	5		
5 Innocence	3		
6 They like group activity	2		
Total	32	Total	11

VOLITIONAL SIDE (61)

1 Quick activities	3	1 Inattentive	17
2 They do not put teacher to much trouble in teaching	2	2 Lack of habit of effort ..	9
		3 After all, they are not firm-spirited children ..	7
		4 Bad habit of disorder ..	6
		5 Put teacher to much trouble in controlling them	6
		6 Talkative	4

THE KINDERGARTEN IN JAPAN

7 Disobedient	4
8 Bad conduct	3

Total 5   Total 56

MISCELLANEOUS (98)

The criticisms offered by teachers in the higher elementary schools, Girls' Higher schools and Middle schools were 37 in number.

HIGHER ELEMENTARY SCHOOL

1 Roughly speaking they belong to the middle class
   in scholarship 1
2 Better marks in arithmetic 2
3 Obedience 1
4 It seems to me that they
   have more ability to play
   than the other group .. 1

1 Too much spirit of de-
   pendence 1
2 They act rashly, not
   thrifty 1
3 No self-possession 1

MIDDLE SCHOOL

1 In my class there are only
   two K.s, both are mild
   and frank 1
2 Among them there are
   some good students ... 1
3 It seems to me all of
   them have better health,
   but, of course, we can
   not say that it is caused
   by the Kindergarten
   training 1
4 Among 126 second-year-
   students there are only
   3 K. s. They all are obe-
   dient and in higher
   standing of moral con-
   duct and scholarship,
   but they have retiring
   disposition and not
   enough vitality 1

1 No effect of Kindergarten 1
2 In general, they are in-
   attentive 1
3 There are many so called
   fast boys among them.. 1
4 In general, they are not
   healthy 1
5 Bad marks in composition 1
6 It seems to me that they
   waste much energy in
   infancy and that is the
   reason why they have
   bad health 1

[57]

These classifications confirm the above-given per-
centage tables, for we find the criticisms which refer
to intellectual aspects are 62 in number, of which 56
favor the K. pupils as contrasted with only 6 against
them. On the other hand, on the volitional side there
are 61 criticisms of which 56 are unfavorable to the
K. pupils. They are declared inferior in attention,
moral traits, orderliness, all of which have been
claimed as special aims of the kindergarten. Kindergarteners who may read this study will, I am sure,
seek to improve their work in these respects if im-
provement is needed.

D. Supplementary Investigation of the School Marks of Kindergarten and NonKindergarten Children

METHOD: This investigation was based on a report
of an elementary school in Tokyo. This school has an
attached kindergarten and the majority of the school
children were, and are, the graduates of the kindergarten. The principal of the school made an interesting report concerning the school marks of 1000 K. and
NK. pupils. Table VII gives these data. The number of the grade children was 1000. The number of
K. was not mentioned in the report. Grading standards were: Very high, A; Medium, B; Low, C. K.
signifies Kindergarten children; NK. Non-Kindergarten children.

[58]

TABLE III

	MORAL						READING					
	K			NK			K			NK		
	A	B	C	A	B	C	A	B	C	A	B	C
I grade	60	37	3	44	49	7	51	46	3	31	58	11
II grade	73	25	2	52	46	2	82	18	0	66	33	11
III grade	41	57	2	27	72	1	41	57	2	28	69	3
IV grade	67	30	3	34	60	6	67	33	0	42	54	4
V grade	53	41	6	45	51	4	47	47	6	36	54	9
Av.	60	37	3	41	55	4	59	40	1	41	53	6

ALL SUBJECTS

K			NK			Ratio of $\frac{NK}{K}$	
A	B	C	A	B	C		
55	43	2	34	57	9	I grade	0.93
67	29	4	49	48	3	II grade	0.95
42	54	4	27	68	5	III grade	0.97
60	37	3	36	56	8	IV grade	0.89
45	46	9	33	59	8	V grade	0.98
55	41	4	36	57	7	Average	0.94

The subjects were 13 in all, i. e., moral, reading, composition, penmanship, arithmetic, drawing, music, gymnastic, manual training, needlework, geography, history and science. To find out the ratio of all the school subjects of NK. and K. the author used the same method which he used in the former investigations, i.e., he found the ratio of $\frac{NK.}{K.}$ In the 1st grade this is 0.93, by following procedure.

$$\frac{34 \times 9 + 57 \times 7 + 9 \times 5}{55 \times 9 + 43 \times 7 + 2 \times 5}$$
$$= 0.93, \text{ etc.}$$

The average ratio of $\frac{NK.}{K.}$ is 0.94. As the reader will understand, this means that if the scholarship of K. were 1 then that of NK. will be .94.

CONCLUSION. This investigation shows obviously that the scholarship of the K. surpasses that of NK.

E. Comparison With Other Investigations

In 1909 Dr. Leonard P. Ayres in New York and in 1911 Supt. Holland, in Louisville, made investigations of the time required by K. and NK. pupils to complete the eight grades. They report no appreciable difference. The investigations made in New Orleans (1914), in Newton, Mass. (1913) and in Kenosha, Wis. (1912) were based upon the length of time taken to complete the work of certain grades. In all three investigations the results were in favor of K. children.

In these investigations the basis of comparison between K. and NK. children has been the length of time required to complete the work of the grades. But the mere speed is only one criterion of educational value.

In Savannah, Carol P. Oppenheimer (1912) made an investigation, based on the school marks of K. and NK. children in the primary grades. The outcome was decidedly in favor of the K. children.

Mr. L. A. Marsh made a study of 380 elementary school children in 12 grades, all of the Edgewood public schools in Pittsburg (1914). The investigation was made with the aid of questionnaires. Teachers were asked to report upon the following points:

1.	Self-confidence	10.	Observation
2.	Moral attitude	11.	Response to direction
3.	Love of nature	12.	Response to ideas
4.	Ability to mix	13.	Manual ability
5.	Friendliness	14.	Cleanliness
6.	Interest	15.	Orderliness
7.	Attention	16.	Oral expression
8.	Ability to think	17.	Ability to play
9.	Originality			

He found that K. children showed greater self-confidence. In moral attitude the NK. surpassed and showed a total difference of 0.33. In love of nature, ability to mix and friendliness K. were ahead; but NK. were far ahead in attention. In all, the NK. surpassed in four points: namely, moral attitude, attention, manual ability and orderliness. The most remarkable differences in favor of K. were in ability to mix, in originality, and in response to ideas. The difference was high in favor of K. in self-confidence, love of nature, friendliness, observation, oral expression, and in ability to play.

F. Conclusions

From these data the author draws the following conclusions: Where K. and NK. children are compared during their progress through the public schools, the kindergarten children are (*a*) superior to non-kindergarten children in scholarship, understanding and memory; roughly speaking K. children are better on the intellectual side; (*b*) inferior in capacity for sustained effort and diligence, (c) inferior in many moral habits, as disorderliness, inattention, talkativeness, disobedience, etc., (*d*) not superior in physical capacity and bodily health.

BIBLIOGRAPHY

CHAPTER I

S. C. PAKER,   "The History of Modern Elementary Education," 1912   433-460

P. MONROE   "Educational Encyclopaedia"   598

F. FROEBEL   "Education of Man," translated by
                W. N. Hailmann.

CHAPTER II

S. C. PAKER   "The History of Modern Elementary Education," 1912   433-460

P. MONROE   "Educational Encyclopaedia"   598

A. C. PERRY   "Outline of School Administration, 1912   55-156

U. S. BULLETIN   "Kindergarten in the U. S.," 1914   7-12-15
No. 6   "The Report of Commission of
U. S.   Education"

CHAPTER III

M. ATSUMA   "The Method of Kindergarten Training" (In Japanese), 1906   120-125

DOBUNKWAN   "Encyclopaedia Japonica" (In Japanese), 1908   1569-1572

CHAPTER IV

G. M. WHIPPLE   "Manual of Mental and Physical Tests," 1914   42-43-44

E. L. THORNDIKE   "Theory of Mental and Social Measurement," 1913   227

INTERNATIONAL   "The Report of the Twenty-Second
KINDERGARTEN   Annual Meeting," 1915   116-117
UNION   "The Elementary School Journal,"
                June No., 1915   543-550

Further references are in the foot-notes.

INDEX TO TABLES

Printed in the USA
CPSIA information can be obtained
at www.ICGtesting.com
LVHW021112281223
767380LV00077B/111